NAVIGATING STORMY SEAS

A RETREAT GUIDE ON JESUS CALMING THE STORM

FR. JOHN BARTUNEK, LC, STHD

ISBN-13: 9798668585458

This booklet is a part of RCSpirituality's *Retreat Guide* service, which includes free online videos and audio tracks available at **RCSpirituality.org**.

INTRODUCTION

We live in a secular age. The word secular comes from a Latin word meaning "this age" or "this world." A secular age is based on the assumption that there is no reality beyond the material reality of this visible universe. It assumes that God, if he exists, is irrelevant to our daily lives, and that true fulfillment must be obtained here and now, no matter the cost.

This secular worldview contradicts the Christian worldview even more than non-Christian religious worldviews do, because the Christian worldview is based on the conviction that what is unseen is actually more intensely real than what is seen, and that our life here on earth is only the first chapter of an adventure that will continue forever into eternity.

Living immersed in a secular culture is hard on our faith. We have to be even more intentional now than in past ages, perhaps, about nourishing and protecting that faith, since the predominant worldview is constantly attacking it. This Retreat Guide, Navigating Stormy Seas, will help us do that:

o   The First Meditation puts us in the boat with Christ's Apostles as they cross the Sea of Galilee and encounter a life-threatening storm.

o   The Second Meditation gives us a chance to explore why Jesus stayed sleeping in the back of the boat while the Apostles were fighting for their lives.

o   And the conference takes us on a tour of church history showing how storms, in the light of God's providence, actually seem to be the norm.

Let's begin, in the quiet of our hearts, by turning our attention to the Lord, who never stops paying attention to us. Let's ask him for all the graces we need, and most especially for the grace to have our faith strengthened and inspired by the living Word of God, just as we find in the fourth chapter of St. Mark's Gospel.

NOTES

FIRST MEDITATION

Asleep Amid the Storm

INTRODUCTION

Let's begin simply by reading the passage from Mark 4 that describes Jesus calming the storm:

> On that day, as evening drew on, he said to them, "Let us cross to the other side." Leaving the crowd, they took him with them in the boat just as he was. And other boats were with him. A violent squall came up and waves were breaking over the boat, so that it was already filling up. Jesus was in the stern, asleep on a cushion. They woke him and said to him, "Teacher, do you not care that we are perishing?" He woke up, rebuked the wind, and said to the sea, "Quiet! Be still!" The wind ceased and there was great calm. Then he asked them, "Why are you terrified? Do you not yet have faith?" They were filled with great awe and said to one another, "Who then is this whom even wind and sea obey?"
>
> —Mark 4:35-41

A REAL CRISIS

Let's be honest: Do the Apostles' actions in this situation seem unreasonable? The situation, after all, was grave.

A good number of the Apostles were fishermen, familiar with boats, the sea of Galilee, and storms. St. Mark makes it abundantly clear that those fishermen were fearing for their very lives. They were not overreacting out of inexperience or ignorance. This was no minor agitation, no minor blip on the weather radar.

Let's pause there and use our imagination to enter more deeply into the experience of the Apostles. Few situations leave men so helpless as storms at sea. When a huge expanse of water rises up against a small fishing boat like they were using, feelings of absolute vulnerability and utter powerlessness often lead to panic or paralysis. The Sea of Galilee, where this event occurred, is still known for the violence of its squalls, which arise and subside rapidly and unpredictably due to its peculiar geographical situation. In the midst of these gales, the forces of nature unleash their full, terrifying power, and human fragility is nakedly exposed.

Most of us have had some kind of similar experience: maybe being lost high on a mountain as daylight was fading; maybe being stranded on a desert highway with an empty tank of gas; maybe being shocked to find ourselves in the middle of a major earthquake; maybe simply being submerged and tumbled around like a small piece of driftwood by a violent, coastal undertow. That sense of precariousness, littleness, and feeble defenselessness brought about by such experiences—the Apostles found themselves in the midst of just that kind of existential crisis.

WHAT WAS JESUS THINKING?

We have to ask ourselves why Jesus allowed that to happen. Why didn't he protect his followers from the storm? Why didn't he give them smooth sailing all the time?

This question touches one of the most profound mysteries of our human condition. Every religion has to grapple with it. Every philosophy has to wrestle with it. And Christianity is no exception.

As Christians, we know that God is all-knowing, all-powerful, all-wise, and all-good. And being all those things, he still allows us to experience the storms of life.

Not all life's storms are meteorological. We can feel our helplessness and be existentially disoriented by other kinds of storms as well: we can be abandoned, betrayed, or even abused by those we love and trust; we can lose a loved one in the prime of life to a crippling disease ; freak accidents can deprive us of those we most care for or need. Horrible scandals can rock our family, our parish, even the Church as a whole. These are just some of the storms that can swamp our boats and bring us to the point where we too, just like the Apostles, are convinced that we can't go on, that we are on the verge of perishing.

PROVIDENCE AND PREVENTION

God allows these things to happen. Certainly, in his providence he also prevents many tragedies and much suffering—we will only know how much prevention his providence has worked when we enter into eternity and are granted a full vision of the story of our lives. And yet, his providence—his all-loving, all-wise, all-powerful providence, doesn't shield us from every storm, just as Jesus didn't shield his Apostles from this storm.

Jesus permits this storm to rock their boat, and he never really gives them a direct answer about why he permits it. Yet, this incident as the Gospels record it adds yet another dimension to this mystery.

St. Mark tells us that in the middle of the storm, Jesus is asleep. This, perhaps more than the storm itself, is what throws the Apostles into confusion. Their leader, their Rabbi, their Lord, the man they had given up everything to follow—he seems to be completely unaware of their suffering. He seems to be oblivious to the storm. He is asleep on a cushion in the back of the boat. They find him there in the middle of the crisis, completely unperturbed. They wake him up and ask him, "Teacher, do you not care that we are perishing?"

DOES JESUS CARE?

These men are fearing for their very lives, and Jesus doesn't even seem to care. They cannot comprehend this. Why doesn't Jesus do something about it? Why doesn't he at least comfort them with some words of wisdom? Why doesn't he guide them in some way as the storm rages on?

This too is an experience we can all relate to, if we are honest. Many times in our Christian journey God seems to be asleep, unaware, uncaring. In times of intense suffering and confusion, he sometimes seems to be absent, silent, aloof. Many times, when we let our hearts speak honestly in prayer, we can only say what the Apostles said as their boat was starting to sink: "Teacher, do you not care that we are perishing?"

At this point in the Gospel of Mark, Jesus had already worked so many amazing miracles and cast out so many demons that "His fame spread everywhere throughout the whole region of Galilee" (Mark 1:28). He had already selected his twelve Apostles as special companions, spending all his time with them and giving them special training and instruction in addition to the teaching he offered to the crowds. They had already witnessed his divine power abundantly, undeniably. They had begun to get to know him personally, deeply. They had heard his preaching and discussed it with him. It doesn't make sense to them that Jesus—their Rabbi who was so powerful, so good, and so faithful—would simply ignore this storm that was threatening to destroy them.

SAILING INTO STORMS

Isn't that exactly our situation as well? We know Jesus, and we have witnessed his power and grace at work in our lives. We know how good and wise he is. And so, when the storms surge and we feel the bitterness of life, we can't reconcile our experience of suffering with our experience of the Lord's loving kindness. So we ask, "Teacher, do you not care that we are perishing?"

In the next meditation, we will dig into the Lord's answer to that question, and what it may have to say to each one of us. But for now, let's take some time, in the quiet of our hearts, to prayerfully reflect on the reality of just how confusing and painful it can be when God allows us to sail into the storm while he sleeps on a cushion in the back of our boat.

QUESTIONS FOR PERSONAL REFLECTION/GROUP DISCUSSION

1. When have I felt myself as desperate and disoriented as the Apostles felt in this midst of this storm? Remember those experiences in the presence of the Lord, not being afraid to ask the Lord an honest, heartfelt question about them, just as the Apostles did.

2. How honestly and deeply have I considered and reflected on God's choice to allow his children to endure terrible storms?

3. How do I usually react when I find myself questioning why God allows certain things? Why?

QUOTATIONS TO HELP YOUR PRAYER

He [Jesus] got into a boat and his disciples followed him. Suddenly a violent storm came up on the sea, so that the boat was being swamped by waves; but he was asleep. They came and woke him, saying, "Lord, save us! We are perishing!" He said to them, "Why are you terrified, O you of little faith?" Then he got up, rebuked the winds and the sea, and there was great calm. The men were amazed and said, "What sort of man is this, whom even the winds and the sea obey?"

—Matthew 8:23–27
NABRE

Meanwhile we have to believe firmly that God calls us to Himself and follows us along the path towards Him. He will never permit anything to happen to us that is not for our greater good. He knows who we are and He will hold out His paternal hand to us during difficulties, so that nothing prevents us from running to Him swiftly. But to enjoy this grace we must have complete trust in Him.

—St. Pio of Pietrelcina

"We cannot accept that salt should become tasteless or the light be kept hidden. The people of today can still experience the need to go to the well, like the Samaritan woman, in order to hear Jesus, who invites us to believe in him and to draw upon the source of living water welling up within him. We must rediscover a taste for feeding ourselves on the word of God, faithfully handed down by the Church, and on the bread of life, offered as sustenance for his disciples. Indeed, the teaching of Jesus still resounds in our day with the same power: "Do not labor for the food which perishes, but for the food which endures to eternal life" (Jn 6:27)… Belief in Jesus Christ, then, is the way to arrive definitively at salvation.

—Apostolic Letter, *Porta Fidei*, 3
POPE BENEDICT XVI

NOTES

SECOND MEDITATION

Why Are We Afraid?

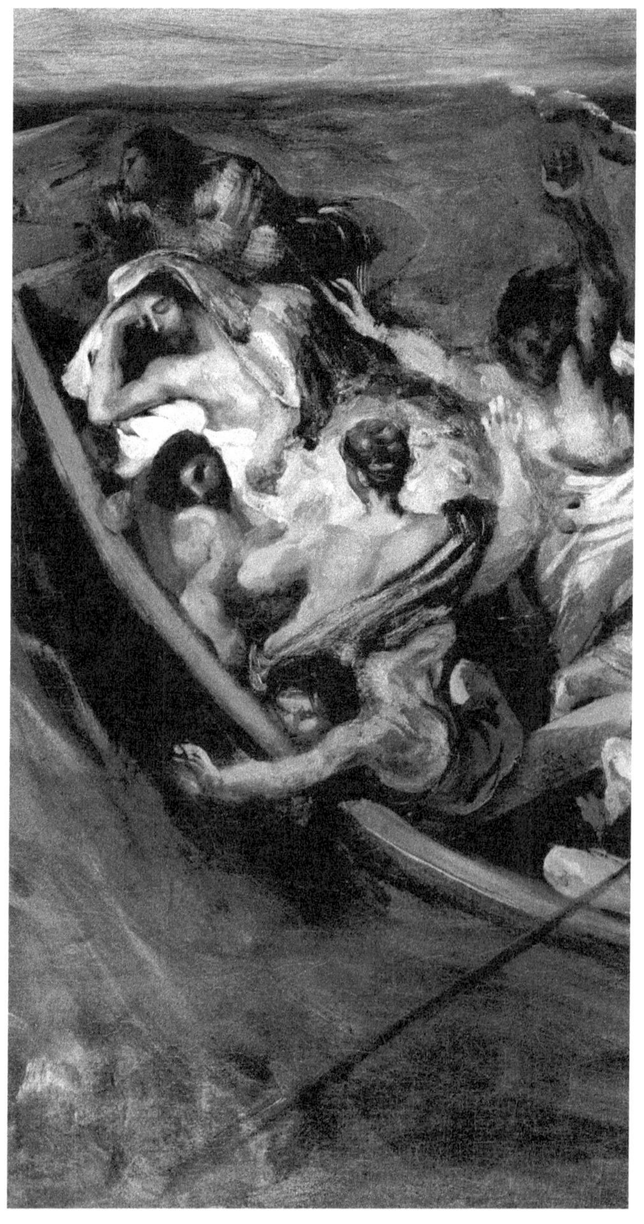

INTRODUCTION

Feeling their lives threatened, completely helpless in the face of nature's awesome power, the Apostles discover that Jesus is asleep in the back of the boat, apparently unaware and uninterested in what could become the greatest crisis of their lives. Filled with urgent confusion, they wake him up, shaking him, and ask, "Teacher, do you not care that we are perishing?"

FISHING FOR AN APOLOGY

In a sense, the Apostles are reprimanding Jesus. They are expressing how hurt and confused they feel. They thought he cared about them. They thought he was a great prophet who would guide and protect them—that's why they gave up everything to become his disciples. They entrusted themselves to him completely, and here he was, unperturbed at their life-threatening crisis.

Maybe they thought he would wake up, drowsily begin to realize the danger they were facing, and say he was so sorry that he had left them alone, and that of course he cares that they are about to perish. Maybe they would even expect him to apologize for having brought them to this point. After all, if he hadn't called them, they wouldn't be in this predicament.

That would have been a logical, human response. It would have made sense to the Apostles. It would make sense to us.

But Jesus didn't apologize. He didn't backtrack. He wasn't ashamed that he had fallen asleep. He didn't regret bringing his followers into this storm.

God doesn't make mistakes. He never needs to apologize. He never fails to live up to his greatness and his faithfulness to us. If we find ourselves in the midst of a storm, that storm will not ruin God's plans for us. He remains all-powerful, all-wise, and all-good, even when we can't see clearly or completely how his power, wisdom, and goodness are at work.

Believing this about God is not, as the skeptics would say, naive or superstitious. The whole Christian mystery revolves around God bringing resurrections out of crucifixions. Crucifixions—storms of injustice and terror in all their forms—are the result of sin, and that was not part of God's original plan for the world and the human race. Sin and the brokenness it introduced into the world are the responsibility of the human family. But God redeems us from sin. God the Father wasn't ignoring his Son's suffering while Jesus hung, tortured and dying, on the Cross. Somehow, he was working out his wonderful plan of salvation. And the Resurrection proves it.

Just so, somehow, that storm on the Sea of Galilee, even while it caused the Apostles fear, and confusion, and dread, and anxiety, was going to become a meaningful thread in the tapestry of salvation history. God doesn't make mistakes. Rather, he turns our mistakes, and even our sins and rebellions, into marvels.

And so, Jesus doesn't apologize. He doesn't justify himself. Because he doesn't need to. He never needs to.

So how does he respond when his Apostles confront him with the accusation "Teacher, do you not care that we are perishing?" Here is what St. Mark tells us:

He woke up, rebuked the wind, and said to the sea, "Quiet! Be still!" The wind ceased and there was great calm. Then he asked them, "Why are you terrified? Do you not yet have faith?"

—Mark 4:39-40

The first thing Jesus does is calm the storm. With a mere word, he rebukes the wind and stills the sea. With this gesture, Jesus shows that the disciples were wrong to doubt his concern. He shows that he does care. And he shows his care by doing something only God could do: He gently tames the immense, wild, destructive, uncontrollable forces of nature, those same forces which just an instant before had starkly exposed the fragility, smallness, and helplessness of the Apostles. Where the Apostles are powerless, the Lord's power is effortless.

GETTING TO KNOW JESUS MORE DEEPLY

The Apostles had already witnessed Jesus's power over illness, through his many miraculous cures. They had already seen his dramatic victories over demonic forces by his authoritative casting out of devils. But now, when he controls nature's majesty with a mere word, they are seeing something new. Because of the storm, they come to know Jesus more deeply than they had known him before. As St. Mark describes it:

They were filled with great awe and said to one another, "Who then is this whom even wind and sea obey?"

—Mark 4:41

Perhaps here we find dramatically presented to us the first and most important reason why God in his wise and loving providence allows storms to batter our lives. In the end, what he wants most is an intimate relationship with us, a friendship with us. And for us to go deeper in our friendship with God, we have to get to know him better. This requires God to reveal himself to us more and more, to push us beyond the limits of our knowledge, limits we often are not even aware of.

In other words, just as the Apostles came to know Christ more fully through their experience of this storm, so too we can come to know God more fully and intimately when we journey with him through experiences that challenge our previous expectations and assumptions, as painful and disorienting as those experiences may be.

DO YOU NOT YET HAVE FAITH?

But Jesus answers his Apostles' question with more than just a gesture, with more than just a miracle. After rebuking the wind and stilling the sea, he turns back to them and asks them a couple questions of his own:

Then he asked them, "Why are you terrified? Do you not yet have faith?"

—Mark 4:40

Jesus seems to be asking these questions rhetorically, in order to show the Apostles why they had been so distraught by the storm. It's as if he is saying, "Do you realize that your fear and anxiety were due simply to your weak faith?"

They believed in Jesus—that is why they had given up everything to follow him. But even after witnessing so many miracles, their faith still had room to grow. Their panic during the storm showed that. They had not yet come to a full understanding of who Jesus was, and of how much Jesus cared for them.

OUR FEARS AND OUR FAITH

Our fears and anxieties flow from the same source. Our reactions to the storms of life show us the reality of our faith, because in them we turn to God just as the Apostles did. But they also show us that our faith has room to grow, because those storms fill us with fear and confusion. They push us beyond our own capacity to control things, and that scares us, because we usually prefer to rely on ourselves rather than on God.

If we respond to these storms as the Apostles did, by going to Jesus, waking him up, and sincerely opening our hearts to him, then, eventually, we too will have the experience of spiritual growth they had as a result of the storm. But for that to happen, we have to hear Jesus asking us: "Why were you terrified? Do you not yet have faith?"

In the Conference, we will look at the history of the Church through the lens of this passage, discovering how being in the midst the storm is, in a certain sense, the normal condition for the Church. But for now, let's take some time, in the quiet of our hearts, to speak freely with our Lord about the state of our faith, and how he may want to help it grow.

QUESTIONS FOR PERSONAL REFLECTION/GROUP DISCUSSION

1. What expectations do I have about how God should treat me? How do I respond when my expectations are not met?

2. In the past, what experiences have helped me get to know God better? When have I grown most in my faith, and what difference did that make for my daily life?

3. What would it look like in my life for me to do what the Apostles did: waking up Jesus who was asleep in the back of the boat and asking him if he cared?

QUOTATIONS TO HELP YOUR PRAYER

❝Enter through the narrow gate; for the gate is wide and the road broad that leads to destruction, and those who enter through it are many. How narrow the gate and constricted the road that leads to life. And those who find it are few… Everyone who listens to these words of mine and acts on them will be like a wise man who built his house on rock. The rain fell, the floods came, and the winds blew and buffeted the house. But it did not collapse; it had been set solidly on rock. And everyone who listens to these words of mine but does not act on them will be like a fool who built his house on sand. The rain fell, the floods came, and the winds blew and buffeted the house. And it collapsed and was completely ruined.

—Matthew 7:13–14, 24–27
NABRE

Your yearning for the peace of eternity is good and holy, but it needs to be balanced by complete submission to divine wishes. It is better to do God's will on earth than to have joy in paradise. St. Teresa's motto was that it was better to suffer than to die. Purgatory is sweet when you suffer out of love for God. The trials that the Lord is giving and will give you are all signs of divine favor and will be jewels for your soul. Dear one, the winter will pass and eternal spring will arrive, and it will be as rich in beauty as the storms were harsh. The fog that you are experiencing is an indication of God's proximity to you.

—St. Pio of Pietrelcina

We may be sure that none of our acts of love will be lost, nor any of our acts of sincere concern for others. No single act of love for God will be lost, no generous effort is meaningless, no painful endurance is wasted. All of these encircle our world like a vital force. Sometimes it seems that our work is fruitless, but mission is not like a business transaction or investment, or even a humanitarian activity. It is not a show where we count how many people come as a result of our publicity; it is something much deeper, which escapes all measurement. It may be that the Lord uses our sacrifices to shower blessings in another part of the world which we will never visit. The Holy Spirit works as he wills, when he wills and where he wills; we entrust ourselves without pretending to see striking results. We know only that our commitment is necessary. Let us learn to rest in the tenderness of the arms of the Father amid our creative and generous commitment. Let us keep marching forward; let us give him everything, allowing him to make our efforts bear fruit in his good time.

—Apostolic Exhortation *Evangelii Gaudium*, #279
POPE FRANCIS

NOTES

CONFERENCE
The Storm Is the Norm

Η CΥΝΟΔΟC ΤΩΝ ΑΓ. ΠΑΤΕΡΩΝ

ΠΙϹΤΕΥΩ ΕΙϹ ΕΝΑ ΘΕΟΝ, ΠΑΤΕΡΑ ΠΑΝΤΟΚΡΑΤΟΡΑ, ΠΟΙΗΤΗΝ ΟΥΡΑΝΟΥ Κ
ΓΗϹ ΟΡΑΤΩΝ ΤΕ ΠΑΝΤΩΝ ΚΑΙ ΑΟΡΑΤΩΝ. ΚΑΙ ΕΙϹ ΕΝΑ ΚΝ ΙΗϹΟΥΝ ΧΝ ΤΟΝ ΥΙΟΝ
ΤΟΥ ΘΥ ΤΟΝ ΜΟΝΟΓΕΝΗ, ΤΟΝ ΕΚ ΤΟΥ ΠΡϹ ΓΕΝΝΗΘΕΝΤΑ ΠΡΟ ΠΑΝΤΩΝ ΤΩΝ ΑΙΩΝΩ
ΦΩϹ ΕΚ ΦΩΤΟϹ ΘΕΟΝ ΑΛΗΘΙΝΟΝ ΕΚ ΘΕΥ ΑΛΗΘΙΝΥ ΓΕΝΝΗΘΕΝΤΑ ΟΥ
ΠΟΙΗΘΕΝΤΑ, ΟΜΟΟΥϹΙΟΝ ΤΩ ΠΡΙ ΔΙ ΟΥ ΤΑ ΠΑΝΤΑ ΕΓΕΝΕΤΟ ΤΟΝ ΔΙ ΗΜΑϹ ΤΟΥϹ
ΑΝΘΡΩΠΥϹ ΚΑΙ ΔΙΑ ΤΗΝ ΗΜΕΤΕΡΑΝ ϹΩΤΗΡΙΑΝ ΚΑΤΕΛΘΟΝΤΑ ΕΚ ΤΩΝ ΟΥΡΑΝΩ
ΚΑΙ ϹΑΡΚΩΘΕΝΤΑ ΕΚ ΠΝϹ ΑΓΙΥ ΚΑΙ ΜΑΡΙΑϹ ΤΗϹ ΠΑΡΘΕΝΥ ΚΑΙ ΕΝΑΝΘ
ΠΗϹΑΝΤΑ. ϹΤΑΥΡΩΘΕΝΤΑ ΤΕ ΥΠΕΡ ΗΜΩΝ ΕΠΙ ΠΟΝΤΙΥ ΠΙΛΑΤΟΥ
ΚΑΙ ΠΑΘΟΝΤΑ, ΚΑΙ ΤΑΦΕΝΤΑ...

INTRODUCTION

The Apostles Creed, the earliest summary of the Christian faith in the history of the Church, has only twelve articles. We still recite it regularly at the beginning of the Rosary. The Nicene-Constantinople Creed, the other ancient, official summary of our faith usually prayed during Mass on Sundays, is a little bit longer than the Apostle's Creed, but it is still based on the original twelve articles of faith.

When written down, the texts of those Creeds can fit on a single piece of paper. But the Universal Catechism of the Catholic Church, the official explanation of our faith, is a thousand pages long. This shows how over the centuries the Church has grown in her understanding of what God revealed to us in Christ. In that sense, the faith of the Church has increased and expanded over the course of the past twenty centuries.

AUTOMATED FAITH?

But that doesn't mean that my faith or your faith is necessarily stronger than the faith of our Christian brothers and sisters from twenty centuries ago. The Church's growth in knowledge about the faith doesn't automatically accumulate in the heart of each believer. The depth, intensity, and vibrancy of any individual believer's faith can't be handed on as easily as mathematical knowledge. Our faith has a moral and spiritual dimension that makes it necessary for every generation, and indeed for every person, to discover and claim it anew. Progress in faith is spiritual progress, linked to spiritual freedom, which is very different from material or technical progress.

In other words, every generation of believers has to go through their own journey of faith, just as the first Apostles did. And so, every generation also has to endure terrible storms, storms that don't seem to make sense, just as the Apostles did. And the Lord will make use of those storms to draw us closer to himself, if we let him.

A HISTORY LESSON

The history of the Church is undeniable proof of that. In our own times, the Church is suffering horribly—persecution, apostasy, and blood-chilling scandals seem to be our daily bread. For those who truly love God and the Church, these storms can be profoundly disorienting, a true trial for our faith, just as the storm on the Sea of Galilee was a true trial for the Apostles' faith.

One way to bolster our faith and keep our hearts firmly anchored in the midst of storms is to remember the crises of our older brothers and sisters in the faith, to remember the storms the Church has endured in the past. This can remind us that God doesn't make mistakes-- that even when he seems to be asleep in the boat and unconcerned with our predicament, he is still loving and protecting us, guiding and sanctifying us.

And in fact, when it comes to the history of the Church, the storm really is the norm. There has never really been a golden age, free from strife, in the history of the Christianity. Every age has faced grave crises that strained people's faith to the breaking point. And in every age, those storms produced saints. The storms of our times can do the same for us. In fact, God is hoping that they will.

Let's take a quick tour through the major periods of Church history, just to show that this is indeed the case.

THE FIRST STORMY CENTURIES

We can start by thinking about the very Apostles themselves. Of the eleven who witnessed the resurrected Christ, ten ended up being martyred. And the organized persecutions under which they suffered rolled over the Church on a regular basis, like the ebbing and flowing of the ocean's tides, throughout the first three centuries of Christianity.

Eusebius, one the Church's first historians and a survivor of the final wave of Roman persecution under the Emperor Diocletian, described the kind of thing that was done to terrorize Christians during those centuries, with a view to stamping out the entire religion:

> In Arabia men were hacked to death. In Cappadocia their legs were cut off. In Mesopotamia some Christians were hung upside-down and suffocated by the smoke of a fire beneath their heads. Sometimes their noses or ears or tongues were cut off. In Pontus the martyrs had pointed reeds driven beneath their finger-nails, and in other cases molten lead was poured over the most sensitive parts of the body.[1]

STORMS OF HERESIES

These persecutions came to an end when the Emperor Constantine legalized and then supported Christianity. But even during his lifetime, new crises sprang up in the form of heresies, especially the Arian heresy, which raged throughout Christendom, violently dividing the Church

---

[1] Quoted in *The Church of the Apostles and Martyrs*, Henri Daniel-Rops, p 411.

from within, pitting bishop against bishop, even at times saint against saint, for more than a hundred years. The theological controversies spawned by Arianism led to the emergence of other heresies, necessitating an ongoing series of ecumenical councils to defend true doctrine.

During these centuries, patriarchs and Byzantine emperors conspired against popes and manipulated episcopal elections, opening the door to controversy and at times violent conflict between Arian Christians and Orthodox Christians. It even led to the abduction and torture of one pope. At certain periods during these centuries the majority of the Church's bishops were actually espousing heresy, while only a minority were preserving and promoting the true Catholic faith. The average faithful Catholic simply didn't know who to trust or where to turn for true Catholic doctrine.

THE STORMS OF THE MIDDLE AGES

After the fall of the Roman Empire in western Europe, the monasteries spearheaded heroic missionary efforts throughout the semi-barbarian kingdoms in England, France, and Germany. Each new monastic foundation and missionary venture ended up being irrigated by the blood of martyrs. And that pattern has continued until the present day.

Sometimes we project the Middle Ages as a golden age for the Church, because of the flourishing of civilization that gradually emerged during the thousand years between St. Augustine and the Italian Renaissance. And yet, every step of progress was accompanied by grim crises, by severe storms.

Here is how one historian describes a particularly corrupt period of Church history known as the Age of Iron, because of the penchant to use daggers instead of diplomacy among both its secular rulers—all professed Christians - and also its ecclesiastics.

> In the forty-three years between 867 and 910, seven Holy Roman Emperors died, and an eighth was blinded by a rival. Of the fifteen Popes during these same years, four were almost certainly murdered; several more may have been murdered; the dead body of one was put on trial - and condemned; and the former wife and daughter of another (who had married before his ordination, and separated after it) were murdered. The Muslims from the south and Vikings from the north, between them, brought fire and sword into almost every corner of Western Europe. Through all of Latin Christendom the fires of faith burned low; saints were few, and those few little known.[2]

Even two hundred years later, when Christian knights from Western Europe took up the cause of the Crusades to liberate the sacred sites of the Holy Land from Muslim control and so once again make the way clear for pilgrims, St. Bernard himself described his age as an age of darkness, dominated by evil:

> Now indeed is the hour of wickedness and the power of darkness. But it is the final hour and the power quickly passes away. Christ the strength of God and the wisdom of God is with us, and he is on our side. Have confidence: he has overcome the world.[3]

---

2   *The Founding of Christendom*, William Carroll, p. 369.

3   St. Bernard's Epistles, 126.6, 14.

Those very Crusades ended in defeat and disaster with the fall of Acre in 1291. In that battle, Muslim armies slaughtered nearly 30,000 inhabitants, including entire convents and friaries. They took another 30,000 prisoners and carted them off to slavery—a stormy finale for a supposed golden age of Christendom.

Towards the end of the Middle Ages, another storm wracked the Church from the inside.

Pope St. Celestine V was elected to the papal throne in 1294. His election came after the Holy See had been vacant for two years, three months, and two days, simply because the twelve cardinals at the time couldn't agree on who should be pope. Imagine how not having a pope for more than two years would have affected the Church. And Pope Celestine turned out to be a bad choice—he voluntarily resigned for ineptitude after only five months and nine days. Soon afterwards, the Great Schism divided Christendom for the majority of the fourteenth century. At one point during the schism, three different men simultaneously claimed to be the legitimate pope, and even future canonized saints didn't agree on which was the real one.

STORMS OF RENAISSANCE AND REFORMATION

We are all familiar with the sexual and political intrigues of the Borgias, the Medicis, and other worldly Renaissance popes. These became the remote cause for one of the greatest crises of all, the Protestant Reformation, which has divided Christians up until the present day, splintering the Body of Christ into hundreds, maybe even thousands, of conflicting denominations and doing inestimable damage to the Church's missionary efforts.

After the religious wars that ravaged Europe in the aftermath of the Reformation, the seed of secularization found fertile soil. At the time of the American Revolution, Pope Pius VI described the resulting cultural malaise in terms that leave no room for doubt about the storm the Church was enduring then:

> Who would not be fearful at the present condition of the Christian people? The divine love by which we abide in God and God in us grows very cold as sins and wickedness increase every day. Who would not be shocked when considering that we have undertaken the task of guarding and protecting the church at a time when many plots are laid against orthodox religion, when the safe guidance of the sacred canons is rashly despised, and when confusion is spread wide by men maddened by a monstrous desire of innovation, who attack the very bases of rational nature and attempt to overthrow them?[4]

That same pope, when he was 81 years old ,was arrested, exiled, and imprisoned by French occupiers, the military arm of the French Revolution Directory. Suffering partial paralysis and infirmity, he was dragged from Rome through Italy and up into Valence, France. One day some visitors told him they admired his courage, and that this epoch of pain and captivity became the fairest moment of an already-celebrated pontificate. Pius VI replied: "This may all be; but what afflicts us is to see the cardinals

---

4   Pope Pius VI, *Encyclical Letter Inscrutabile*, #2 (1775).

dispersed and persecuted. How is our poor Rome, so dear to our heart? What has become of our beloved people? What is the future of the Church of God, which we are about to leave so rent and tossed?"[5]

MODERN STORMS

A few decades later, although the excesses of the French Revolution had been reined in, Blessed Pope Pius IX was still able to describe the situation of the Church and the world in truly apocalyptic terms:

When we contemplate the whole Catholic world with the care and affection of our apostolic love, we can hardly put into words how deeply saddened we are at seeing Christian and civil society disturbed and thoroughly confused, oppressed and torn apart by all kinds of disasters. Moreover, you know very well how the Christian people are afflicted and harassed by ferocious wars, internal discords, plagues, earthquakes, and other serious troubles. In addition, it is lamentable that among so many injuries and evils perpetrated by the sons of darkness, who are more artful than the sons of light, they try energetically to wage a bitter war against the Catholic Church and its doctrines. In this they use diabolic deceits, arts, and labors. They attempt to overthrow the authority of the Church's legitimate power and to corrupt the minds and souls of everyone.[6]

---

5   Cf. Artaud de Montor, *The Lives and Times of the Popes.*

6   Pope Pius IX, *Encyclical Letter Apostolicae Nostrae Caritatis,* #1 (1854).

We could multiply quotations like that from every period of Church history, including the harrowing descriptions of persecution in the twentieth century by communists, Nazis, and Fascists alike.

A STORMY PLAN OF REDEMPTION

The point of taking time to review this litany of misery is not to discourage us. Rather, it is to illustrate how God has chosen to unfold his plan of redemption. Although he surely shields his faithful from many storms, he doesn't shield us from all storms. And it seems that in his yearning for us to grow in our faith, to deepen our friendship with him by coming to know more deeply and more fully his infinite wisdom, goodness, and power, he has permitted storms to be the Church's normal habitat.

As we saw in the meditations, God knows what he is doing. He doesn't make mistakes. And so, in the midst of our darkest times and our wildest disorientation, we should feel free to go to the back of the boat and try to wake Jesus up with the cries of our heart. Jesus will surely give us what we need to continue loving, hoping, and believing, and when we do, we will fulfill our mission in the world, whether or not we ever see the fruits of it on this side of eternity.

Pope Francis emphasized the need for faith in the midst of storms in his apostolic exhortation on proclaiming the Gospel in today's world:

> Faith also means believing in God, believing that he truly loves us, that he is alive, that he is mysteriously capable of intervening, that he does not abandon

us and that he brings good out of evil by his power and his infinite creativity… Let us believe the Gospel when it tells us that the kingdom of God is already present in this world and is growing, here and there, and in different ways: like the small seed which grows into a great tree… Because we do not always see these seeds growing, we need an interior certainty, a conviction that God is able to act in every situation, even amid apparent setbacks...[7]

God knows what he is doing. When we don't understand, we can take comfort in knowing that our brothers and sisters in the faith who have gone before us have also had their faith tested, from apostolic times through post-modern times, and they found that God truly was faithful.

Take some time now to prayerfully consider the questions in the personal questionnaire, which are designed to help you apply these general truths to your particular situation.

PERSONAL QUESTIONNAIRE

1. How familiar am I with the storms suffered by the Church throughout its history?

2. In the midst of my own storms, how often do I call to mind the experience of Christians who have gone before me in order to find light, comfort, and strength?

3. In my own words, how would I explain why God permits his Church to suffer through so many storms?

---

7   Pope Francis, *Apostolic Exhortation Evangelii Gaudium*, 278-279.

4. How would I explain to someone else why I believe that God guides his Church, even when it has suffered so much corruption through the centuries?

5. How do I react to the news of scandals in the Church today? How should my faith inform that reaction?

6. How much time and mental energy do I spend uselessly complaining about things that go wrong? How could I better invest that time and mental energy?

7. What am I doing on a regular basis to strengthen my faith?

8. What am I doing on a regular basis to help strengthen the faith of others?

9. In what ways does secularism—the worldview that seeks total happiness here and now, apart from Christ and sharing in his Cross and the hope of heaven—affect my thinking on a day-to-day basis? In what ways does it affect my reactions to storms?

10. Who inspires me as a model for authentic Christian faith? How can I better tap into the inspiration that person gives me?

NOTES

FURTHER READING

Under the Mercy
by Sheldon Vanauken

Inside the Passion
by Fr. John Bartunek, LC

*Stumbling Blocks or Stepping Stones: Spiritual Answers
to Psychological Questions*
by Benedict J. Groeschel, CFR

Darkness in the Marketplace
by Thomas Green, SJ

*The Church in Crisis: A History of the
General Councils 325-1870*
by Philip Hughes

Come Rack! Come Rope!
by Robert Hugh Benson

Please visit our website, *RCSpirituality.org*, for more spiritual resources, and follow us on Facebook for regular updates: *facebook.com/RCSpirituality.*

If you would like to support and sponsor a Retreat Guide, please consider making a donation at RCSpirituality.org.

Retreat Guides are a service of Regnum Christi.
RegnumChristi.org

Produced by Coronation Media.
CoronationMedia.com

Developed & Self-published by RCSpirituality.
RCSpirituality.org